21st Century Junior Library

RECOGNIZING AND MANAGING STRESS

Read and Reflect: A Social-Emotional Guide

Emily Rose

Published in the United States of America by:

CHERRY LAKE PRESS
2395 South Huron Parkway, Suite 200, Ann Arbor, Michigan 48104
www.cherrylakepress.com

Reading Adviser: Beth Walker Gambro, MS, Ed., Reading Consultant, Yorkville, IL
Photo Credits: © Prostock-studio/Shutterstock.com, cover, 1, 5; © Onchira Wongsiri/Shutterstock.com, 6; © Krakenimages.com/Shutterstock.com, 7, 11 [bottom, right], 16; © Matthias G. Ziegler /Shutterstock.com, 8, 9; © Asier Romero/Shutterstock.com, 10; © Luis Molinero/Shutterstock.com, 11 [top], 11 [bottom, left]; © XiXinXing/Shutterstock.com, 12; © Sudowoodo/Shutterstock.com, 13; © Roman Samborskyi/Shutterstock.com, 15; © Monkey Business Images/Shutterstock.com,18; © Laugesen Mateo/Shutterstock.com, 19; © GOLFX/Shutterstock.com, 20

Cherry Lake Press is an imprint of Cherry Lake Publishing Group.

Library of Congress Cataloging-in-Publication Data

Names: Rose, Emily (School psychologist), author.
Title: Recognizing and managing stress / by Emily Rose.
Description: Ann Arbor, Michigan : Cherry Lake Publishing, [2022] | Series: Read and reflect: a social-emotional guide | Includes bibliographical references and index. | Audience: Grades 2-3
Identifiers: LCCN 2021036749 (print) | LCCN 2021036750 (ebook) | ISBN 9781534199118 (hardcover) | ISBN 9781668900253 (paperback) | ISBN 9781668906019 (ebook) | ISBN 9781668901694 (pdf)
Subjects: LCSH: Stress management—Juvenile literature. | Stress (Psychology)—Juvenile literature. | Stress in children—Juvenile literature.
Classification: LCC BF575.S75 R657 2022 (print) | LCC BF575.S75 (ebook) | DDC 155.9/042–dc23
LC record available at https://lccn.loc.gov/2021036749
LC ebook record available at https://lccn.loc.gov/2021036750

Cherry Lake Press would like to acknowledge the work of the Partnership for 21st Century Learning, a Network of Battelle for Kids. Please visit http://www.battelleforkids.org/networks/p21 for more information.

Printed in the United States of America
Corporate Graphics

CHERRY LAKE PRESS

CONTENTS

WHAT IS STRESS AND WHAT DOES IT FEEL LIKE?

Have you ever heard someone say they were feeling "**stressed** out?" Stress is your body's reaction to response to an **emotional** event or situation. You might show stress in your body by **clenching** your jaw or fists, frowning, or having a headache or stomachache. Your heart might beat really fast, or your muscles may feel so tight that you can't relax. Stress can also affect your mind with worried, **nervous**, or **negative** thoughts.

What does the word "stress" mean to you?

Stress can feel different for different people. You can learn about how you feel stress. When you notice you feel stressed out, take a deep breath and pay attention to how your body feels and what your mind is thinking. Then the

What thoughts come into your mind when you feel stressed?

next time your body or your mind feels those things, you'll recognize that these are clues that you feel stressed. These clues will help you do something about it.

Think!

Think of a time when you felt stressed. Do you think this was good stress that helped keep you safe? Or was it bad stress that made you too worried to try something new that wasn't dangerous?

GOOD STRESS AND BAD STRESS

Stress is not all bad. Sometimes we feel stressed or nervous before trying something new. Your brain is on high alert during these times. It hasn't **experienced** that thing yet, and it might not know what to expect. Stress can be a signal that your brain and body need some attention to return back to normal or **regulate**.

When do you feel stress?

Stress has a long history. When humans lived in groups as hunters and **gatherers**, stress helped them respond to very real dangers. For example, if a person saw a lion, he would feel stress. That feeling would **motivate** his body to take action by running to safety. That was good stress,

How do you feel in your body when you feel stressed?

because it quickly resulted in an action that kept that person safe.

Today we feel stress for real situations, like moving to a new city or going to the dentist. But just because something makes you feel stress doesn't mean that it's truly dangerous. You might even feel stress about things that you imagine could happen. Your brain

tries to think of all **possibilities** that could happen in order to plan how to keep you safe in any situation. That's a helpful thing for our brains to do, but it isn't helpful if our brains are doing this type of worrying or stressing all the time.

Stressful thoughts about things you imagine *could* happen but probably aren't *really* going to happen take up space and energy in your brain. Stress isn't good when you feel it all the time. That's when stress and worried thinking can impact our life and **prevent** us from doing things that we might really enjoy.

Make a Guess!

Now that you know some stress can be good, how do you think good stress can help you?

Has there been a time when stress stopped you from doing something you were excited about?

What are some things you can do to prevent stress?

HOW TO MANAGE STRESS

Different people feel stress in different ways. This means that different people respond to stress differently too! You might like to take a nap when you feel stressed, while your mom might like to take long walks outside. Everyone can try different things to find out what works best for their own brain and body.

Preventative **strategies** are things you do to take care of yourself each day so that your body and mind are less likely to feel stressed out in the first place. These things include getting enough sleep, exercising, spending time with friends and family, and eating healthy foods.

What's your favorite way to exercise?

Strategies that can help in the moment when you feel stressed include deep breathing or focusing on relaxing each muscle in your body one at a time. You can also try talking to someone you trust, writing down your worried thoughts and then tearing them up, or **distracting** yourself with something fun, like taking a walk or coloring a picture.

Ask Questions!

What are some things you can try that can help **reduce** stress in the moment when you really feel it? Ask a friend or adult how they reduce stress.

EXTEND YOUR LEARNING

Let's take a moment to imagine the last time you felt stressed.

Write about what made you feel stressed. Was it a test, a fight with a friend or family member, or feeling left out of an activity?

Now think about how you felt that stress. Did you clench your jaw or feel like you had a headache? Did you feel sweaty or dizzy?

What helped you to feel better during this situation? Maybe your teacher offered you kind words, such as "You can do it." Maybe you took some deep breaths in and out until you felt calmer.

Sometimes different strategies help reduce stress in different situations. For example, writing down your thoughts might help you if your mind is full of worried thoughts. However, this strategy might not work if you are in class and supposed to be working on something else.

Now think about the situations where you find yourself feeling stressed most often. Use the ideas mentioned above to make a plan to manage stress in each of those situations. For example, if you often feel stressed before a swim meet, brainstorm ideas that you can use before each meet to help prevent or manage stress. You might want to try listening to calming music or doing deep breathing exercises. Remember, when you control your stress, it doesn't control you!

GLOSSARY

clenching **(CLENCH-ing)** closing tightly

distracting **(dih-STRAKT-ing)** something that directs your attention elsewhere

experienced **(ik-SPEER-ee-uhnst)** done or occurred

emotional **(ih-MOH-shuh-nuhl)** having to do with feelings

gatherers **(GAH-thuhr-urz)** people who collect food, usually plants

motivate **(MOH-tuh-vayt)** encourage

negative **(NEH-guh-tiv)** unfavorable, not positive

nervous **(NUR-vuhss)** uneasy or worried

possibilities **(pah-suh-BIH-luh-teez)** things that could happen

prevent **(prih-VENT)** keep something from happening

reduce **(rih-DOOS)** to make less

regulate **(REH-gyuh-layt)** to control or to return to normal

strategies **(STRAH-tuh-jeez)** plans of action

stressed **(STREST)** affected by stress or worry

FIND OUT MORE

Books

Cook, Julia. *Wilma Jean the Worry Machine.* Chattanooga, TN: National Center for Youth Issues, 2021.

Romain, Trevor, and Elizabeth Verdick. *Stress Can Really Get on Your Nerves.* Minneapolis, MN: Free Spirit Publishing, 2017.

Websites

YouTube—Coping Skill Ideas for Elementary School Kids

https://www.youtube.com/watch?v=B3wsY138qOI
Learn some coping skills to help manage your stress.

YouTube—Stress Explained: Elementary Edition

https://www.youtube.com/watch?v=k8FiAxAqqYE
Watch this video to learn how stress affects your body.

INDEX

ABOUT THE AUTHOR

Emily Rose is a school psychologist, yoga teacher, and writer for her mental wellness blog, MissMagnoliaSays.com. She enjoys helping kids and adults understand and manage their emotions and live beautiful lives. Emily lives in Dearborn, Michigan.